The FUNbook of Creative Writing

REM 104D

Another Teaching Resource from...

RP
REMEDIA
PUBLICATIONS

BLACKLINE MASTERS

Written by Dennis E. Paul
Illustrations by Danny Beck
Captions by Dan W. Deacon

To find Remedia products in a store near you, contact:
www·rempub·com/stores

Remedia Publications, Inc. • 15887 N. 76 Street • Suite 120 • Scottsdale, AZ 85260

ABOUT THE BOOK

The attention-getting, humorous story starters in this book will surely spark the imagination of the most reluctant story writer. The antics of characters with unusual names will motivate young writers to complete the stories and even create their own stories about the subjects. Reading Level is 3.5–4.5.

ABOUT THE AUTHOR

Dennis Paul has been an educator for over twenty years. He taught for eleven years in a one-room school, working with students in grades K-8. He also has served as a special education teacher in a school for homeless students, and as a teacher for acute care adolescent hospital programs.

Currently, he is a special education teacher for the Juvenile Detention Facility in Mesa, Arizona. For many years, he has been creating math word problems, story starters, games, and other materials, to help motivate his own students.

SUGGESTIONS

Below are suggestions for expanded use of the *FUNbook of Creative Writing*.

✔ Have students share their stories with the class through oral reading.

✔ Place students together to create a cooperative story.

✔ Help students spin off the story ideas to create original plots.

✔ Have the whole class brainstorm ideas for various conclusions to a story.

✔ The teacher underlines selected words in students' stories and has them find synonyms for those words (as a vocabulary enrichment activity).

✔ Divide students into groups to create dialogue for the characters and then act out the story for the class.

✔ Have students draw original artwork relating to each story written.

✔ Collect each writer's own stories in an individual Fun Folder of Creative Writing.

_____
[story title]

Herb Waffle woke up one morning to find that all his neighbors were standing on the sidewalk in front of his house. They were carrying signs and looked very angry. One of the signs read, "No More Sheep!" Another read, "Herb Waffle Move Out Now!"

Herb has 72 sheep in his front yard. Recently he had planned to buy 28 more. He decided to get dressed and go out to talk to his angry neighbors. Maybe he could tell them something to make them forget about being angry. As he got dressed, he began to think of something to say. When he went outside, he suddenly shouted... [finish the story]

_____

_____

_____

_____

_____

_____

_____

_____

_____

_____

_____

_____

_____
[story title]

Oscar Hudnut was really excited! He was driving to his new job.
He is supposed to watch all of the sheep on Arnold's Sheep Ranch. "Wow!"
he thought, "I can't believe I am going to be watching all the sheep at
Arnold's ranch. What an easy job this will be. There are 6,779,002 sheep
at the ranch, but all they do is eat all day. How could any of them get into
trouble just doing that?"

He drove up to the ranch and got out of his car. "Look at all the
sheep," he said out loud. "This is going to be fun!" [finish the story]

_____

_____

_____

_____

_____

_____

_____

_____

_____

_____

[story title]

Lulu Lumpit delivers chickens to restaurants and chicken ranches. One day she had a load of 50,513 chickens she had to deliver to Chuck's Fine Food Cafe. It's located on Highway 99, which is very busy. As she was driving, she thought of all the chickens she had delivered over the past 10 years. "I really do deliver a lot of chickens," she thought. Just then, as she checked the traffic in her rearview mirror, she thought she saw a chicken looking at her. "That's strange," she thought. "For a minute, it looked like a chicken was looking at me. They usually don't pay any attention to me." She looked up and saw two chickens looking at her. "Gee," she thought, "I wonder what they are thinking?" [finish the story]

_____

_____

_____

_____

_____

_____

_____

_____

_____

_____

_____
[story title]

Carl Gargle has a 200-pound cat named Snowball. He was on his way to buy a new kitchen window. Snowball had thrown his food dish through the window when he discovered that Carl had bought some cheap cat food instead of his favorite. Carl has had a lot of trouble with Snowball. For instance, last week he ate a pair of Carl's favorite shoes. "I don't know what I am going to do with Snowball," he thought. "He is costing me a lot of money. I have to figure out a way to make Snowball behave more like a normal cat." [finish the story]

_____

_____

_____

_____

_____

_____

_____

_____

_____

_____

Name _____

[story title]

Herb Fern is a very rich man. He has $600,000,000.47 in the bank. He doesn't like to spend a lot of money on his clothes or his car. He likes to buy bread that is a few days old. He always reads the newspaper at the library so he doesn't have to buy his own copy.

Something was about to happen that would change Herb's life forever! He was in the bank, checking on his money, when the manager of the bank walked up and... [finish the story]

_____

_____

_____

_____

_____

_____

_____

_____

_____

_____

_____

_____

_____

_____

_____
[story title]

Oscar Fafner loves living on the 78th floor of his apartment building. He likes the view of the city, the fresh air, and his quiet neighbors. He loves everything about his apartment, except for one thing. The elevator in his building has been broken for six years. It takes him five hours a day just to walk down and back up the stairs. "I have to find a new way to get back up to my apartment," he said one day. "I am sick of walking up and down all these stairs!" He began to think of some way to solve this problem. Then one day, he had an idea. He... [finish the story]

_____

_____

_____

_____

_____

_____

_____

_____

_____

_____

_____

_____

_____

Name _____

_____
[story title]

Wilma Bing was not a happy camper. She and her cat, Randolph, were camping by Lake Fuzzner. She loved to come up to the mountains and camp, but now she was surrounded by hundreds of other tents. There were radios blaring, and people were playing football. It was so noisy that Wilma couldn't hear a bird even if it sat on her shoulder and chirped into your ear! Randolph wasn't happy either. Wilma usually had to watch Randolph very carefully when they were at home. He was always getting into trouble. "I wish I could hear the peaceful sounds of the forest instead of all this noise," she said. She looked at Randolph. Randolph looked at her. Wilma began to think of a plan... [finish the story]

_____

_____

_____

_____

_____

_____

_____

_____

_____

_____

_____

[story title] _____

"When I decided to become the first person to hop across the United States," thought Melvin Noggle, "I don't know what I was thinking!" Melvin Noggle was in Pennsylvania, about 10 miles from Pittsburgh. He was hopping along Highway 24, and he was exhausted! His sister, Nina, was riding behind him in a van with the words "Melvin Noggle Hops Across America" in big red letters.

Each night, Melvin slept inside the van. Nina made sure he drank enough water during the day. Each morning, he had to get up and start hopping. Melvin had been hopping for a month, and they still had a long way to go. "Oh, well," Melvin thought, "at least Pennsylvania is kind of flat." He looked at the highway stretched out in front of him. "At least there aren't any dogs like the ones that started chasing me in New Jersey!"

As he hopped along, he thought he saw a few dark clouds in the distance. [finish the story]

_____

_____

_____

_____

_____

_____

_____

_____

[story title]

Nick Muldoon is very happy. He is on a two-week vacation and he is driving to Pelican Beach. He needs this vacation because he works at the Ace Dynamite Factory. He has to make sure that all of the dynamite is safely packed into boxes before it's loaded onto trucks to be shipped. He needs a lot of peace and quiet. Pelican Beach is usually a very quiet place. He always goes there on his vacation because there are no noisy crowds, no loud noises, no loud music, and, especially, no fireworks. Even the seagulls are quiet.

As he arrived at the Pelican Beach Hotel and began to take his suitcase out of his car, he thought he heard... [finish the story]

_____

_____

_____

_____

_____

_____

_____

_____

_____

_____

_____

_____
[story title]

Duffy Ziltch was looking at the clock. "Oh great," he said, "it's almost 5:00 and I can't wait to go home!" Duffy runs the Lost and Found Department at the Bovine City Bus Station. It was packed with all the items people leave behind on buses. He had suitcases, eyeglasses, bowling balls, false teeth, birdcages, and even a piano. Just as Duffy was about to turn off the lights, Nelson Noodle, the bus driver who usually drives the bus to Walrus Falls, came through the door.

"Duffy, don't close up yet! I have something here that someone left behind on my bus." Duffy couldn't see what Nelson was holding because he backed into the room. Nelson suddenly turned around, and there in his arms was a very large chimpanzee.

"Hey!" Duffy shouted, "You can't bring a monkey in here!"

[finish the story]

_____
_____
_____
_____
_____
_____
_____
_____
_____

_____
[story title]

Sally Sneed is a scientist. She studies the plants that grow in cold climates. A month ago, Sally received a letter from Dr. Lester Lumpit, a world-famous scientist. The letter said:

"Dear Sally, I have discovered something very strange in the mountains of Antarctica. Would you be interested in coming to Antarctica? I need your help with a new discovery.   Sincerely, Dr. Lester Lumpit P.S.: Please hurry!"

Sally made plans to go right away. After traveling by jet, she finally reached Antarctica. Dr. Lumpit met her at the airport. They decided to travel to the mountains the next morning to see the new discovery.

As they rode to the mountains on snowmobiles, Dr. Lumpit said, "I am so glad you are here, Sally. I've never seen anything like this in all the years I have worked here. I never thought I would see a giant..."

[finish the story]

_____
_____
_____
_____
_____
_____
_____
_____
_____

_____
[story title]

Nelson Noodle was driving his bus back to the Bovine City Bus Station. Suddenly his beeper went off. He looked down at the tiny display and read the message, "See the boss when you get back." When he got back, he knocked on the door, which was half open. "You wanted to see me, Mrs. Ginch?" Nelson asked nervously.

"Nelson, please sit down. I have a job for you...an unusual job," she said as she swiveled around in her big chair. "A group of magicians is having an annual convention right here in Bovine City," she continued, "and they want a bus to take them around to see all the sights. Will you do it?" she asked.

"Well, I guess it wouldn't be too tough driving some magicians around," he said. "Sure, Mrs. Ginch, I'll do it." [finish the story]

_____

_____

_____

_____

_____

_____

_____

_____

_____

12

_____
[story title]

Arnold Sharpel works at Dave's Superhighway Hotel on Highway 99. He used to work in the laundry room and was responsible for washing all the towels. He did such a good job, he was promoted to assistant manager. Arnold was a little worried because the manager, Elmo Flecktone, was going on vacation. Arnold would be in charge of the hotel for two weeks. Elmo had told him not to worry, but Arnold began to think of all the things that could possibly go wrong.

"What if the electricity goes off?" he thought. "What if there is an accident or lots of people start to complain about the food or their rooms?" It was 9:00 in the morning and Arnold was behind the front desk. Everything was going fine and Arnold was beginning to relax. Just then a huge bus pulled up in the parking lot. **[finish the story]**

_____

_____

_____

_____

_____

_____

_____

_____

_____

_____

_____
[story title]

There was news at the Ace Bowling Ball Factory. Arney Beagle, who drills holes into the bowling balls, had heard that the company was going to make a big announcement. As he pulled into the parking lot, he saw Arnel Wheese, the president of the Ace Bowling Ball Company. Mr. Wheese began to speak, "We have decided to buy a new machine, the Winsock 2000 Bowling Ball Drilling Robot which will be controlled by a huge computer. This robot will drill all the holes in our bowling balls from now on! I also want to announce that I am giving Arney Beagle a new job. He will be in charge of the Winsock 2000 Bowling Ball Drilling Robot."

Arney did not know what to say. He did not want to be in charge of a computer that was taking over his job. He did not know what to do.

[finish the story]

_____

_____

_____

_____

_____

_____

_____

_____

_____

[story title]

The Bovine City Restaurant is very busy. Pearl Magillicuty is the manager and cook at the restaurant. There is another restaurant in town. It's called Jake's Fine Food, but most people go to the Bovine City Restaurant because they like Pearl's cooking. Lately, some strange things have been going on. Someone left little cards on some of the seats. They read, "The food in this restaurant is no good! Save your money!   ...A friend"

"Who could be leaving these cards?" Pearl wondered. She was in the kitchen chopping all the cabbages so she could cook some cabbage soup. It was usually the Tuesday Night Special at the Bovine City Restaurant. As she was chopping, she noticed a note inside one of the cartons of cabbages. It said, "Give up now or else!"

Pearl was worried now. Who could be doing this? [finish the story]

_____

_____

_____

_____

_____

_____

_____

_____

[story title]

Nelson Noodle is a bus driver for the Bovine City Bus Company. He was driving on the highway and he was thinking, "I wish something exciting would happen."

Suddenly he noticed an old man standing by the side of the road carrying a big package. He was waving one hand to flag down the bus. Nelson stopped the bus. The man had on a huge, gray overcoat and he wore a hat pulled down over his eyes.

"Going to Walrus Falls, mister?" Nelson asked. The man stepped up onto the bus carrying the big package. "That will be $3.75, please." Nelson held out his hand. The man took out his wallet, gave Nelson the money, and quickly took a seat near the back.

"That's strange," Nelson thought. "He never said a word. I wonder why he is carrying that huge package." [finish the story]

_____

_____

_____

_____

_____

_____

_____

_____

Name _____

_____
[story title]

$\mathbf{B}$iff Wigget operates a huge bubble gum cutting machine at the Ace Bubble Gum Factory. He was working one day when an announcement came over the loudspeaker. "May I have your attention please!" it boomed. "I have the great pleasure of announcing that Ace Bubble Gum Factory has been bought by Luther Lugnut's Mega Farms! As you know, it is the largest producer of synthetic vegetable flavors. Together we plan to bring out a new line of bubble gum called Vitagum. It will be available in the following flavors: spinach, broccoli, carrot, corn, and brussel sprout. I know you will continue to do a fine job for me and for Luther Lugnut!" [finish the story]

_____

_____

_____

_____

_____

_____

_____

_____

_____

_____

_____

_____

_____
[story title]

Smiley Furnoose used to raise cattle in his garage. Unfortunately, his neighbors were very unhappy living next door to cattle, so he had to move. His new ranch is called the Lazy B and he has a lot of cattle. Last year he had 50,000 steers, cows, and calves. Nino Giblet is the ranch manager. It is his job to see that all the cattle are rounded up and counted.

Smiley was in the ranch office when Nino came running in. "Boss, I can't believe it! I don't know how to tell you this. The boys and I were going to count the cattle, but... Boss, they are all gone!" [finish the story]

_____

_____

_____

_____

_____

_____

_____

_____

_____

_____

[story title]
_____

Gloria Gussit fixes all the dishwashers, washing machines, refrigerators, and microwaves at Linda Bink's Fix-It Shop. She was known all over Bovine City as the person to call if you have a problem with an appliance.

Gloria and Linda were in the shop when the phone rang. "Linda Bink's Fix-It Shop, Linda Bink speaking." Linda always answered the phone. "You want Gloria Gussit to come *where*? ...to fix what? Is this some kind of joke?" Linda shouted into the phone. "Sure I'll tell her ... uh huh ... okay... goodbye." Linda sat down at her desk. She reached over and flipped a switch on the intercom so she could speak to the people in the shop. "Gloria, you better come to the office. I just got a call from The White House! They want you to fix the presidential microwave! They're sending a helicopter here now." [finish the story]

_____

_____

_____

_____

_____

_____

_____

_____

_____

_____

_____
[story title]

Lulu Werble delivers all the mail in town. She has worked for the post office for 10 years. She is also a deputy sheriff, a member of the volunteer fire department, a private investigator for the Open Eyes Detective Agency, and a former trapeze performer for Zlinger Brothers Circus. She was on her mail route, walking down East Clinker Street, when she noticed a strange truck parked about two houses down. "Sid's Socks Are the Very Best! Put Your Feet in Our Socks!" was written in big red letters along the back and on both sides of the truck. "That's strange," thought Lulu, "Sid's Sock Shop is closed for two weeks. Sid asked me to hold all his mail because he's going to visit his Uncle Chester in Freezing Hands, North Dakota. I better have a closer look at that truck!"

[finish the story]

_____

_____

_____

_____

_____

_____

_____

_____

_____

_____

_____
[story title]

    Vern Lobbit is the gardener at Ajax Elementary School. His biggest job is mowing the lawn all around the school. It takes him 24 hours because the lawn and the football field are huge. He was riding on his mower cutting the grass when he looked down and saw a large hole. There was a pile of dirt next to the hole, a really big pile. As he shut his mower off and walked toward the hole, he noticed the other holes that were hidden by the tall grass. There were at least a dozen giant holes with dirt beside them. Vern looked down into one of the holes. "I wonder what kind of animal made these?" he thought nervously. "It can't be gophers... unless the gophers are the size of my dining room table!" [finish the story]

_____

_____

_____

_____

_____

_____

_____

_____

_____

_____

_____

_____
[story title]

The Open Eyes Detective Agency gets a lot of calls. Lulu Werble works as a private investigator. She also delivers the mail, is a firefighter, a deputy sheriff, and a former trapeze performer. She was in the office when the phone rang. "Open Eyes Detective Agency. How can we help you?" she said.

"Hello... this is Nino Feeney. Is this Lulu?" he asked quickly.

"Yes, this is Lulu; what's the problem?" she asked.

"Well, you see, I don't have a car so I ride my bicycle to my job at the Donut Factory. It's 116 miles away, so I have to start riding when it is still dark."

"Okay, but how can we help you?" Lulu questioned.

"I need you to find out who is trying to run me off Highway 99 every morning at about 6:15!" [finish the story]

_____

_____

_____

_____

_____

_____

_____

_____

Name _____

[story title]

Erleen Splurge and her goldfish, Buster, are one of the most popular acts in the Zlinger Brothers Traveling Circus. Buster is the world's largest and heaviest goldfish. He weighs 16 pounds and measures 25 inches from nose to tail. Erleen has had Buster since he was a tiny goldfish. She enjoys showing Buster to all the people. He even does a few tricks.

For the last few days, Erleen has noticed a change in Buster. Usually Buster swims around his tank and does a few jumps when Erleen comes into the room. Now Buster just swims in place and looks at Erleen. Usually Buster has a great appetite and eats all the food Erleen sprinkles into the tank. Now, Buster just takes a few bites and looks sad.

"I wonder what is wrong with Buster?" Erleen thought, "I wonder why he looks so sad?" [finish the story]

_____

_____

_____

_____

_____

_____

_____

_____

_____

_____

_____
[story title]

The annual Walrus Falls Bowl-O-Rama starts in two days. The best bowlers from everywhere will compete. Chester Bigalow is the best bowler in Walrus Falls. He always wins the Bowl-O-Rama.

Chester was practicing when he noticed a newspaper someone had left behind. It was open to an article about the Walrus Falls Bowl-O-Rama. Chester picked it up and read: "An unknown bowler has entered the annual Walrus Falls Bowl-O-Rama. Nothing is known about him and he has refused all interviews. Our sources tell us he is very, very good. Chester Bigalow is going to have a tough job winning again this year."

Chester sat down. He began to feel a little nervous. "I wonder who this new contestant is?" he thought. He decided to practice a lot more!

[finish the story]

_____

_____

_____

_____

_____

_____

_____

_____

_____

_____

_____
[story title]

The busiest place on Highway 99 is Nino and Gus's Hubcaps Galore. Nino and Gus polish hubcaps and replace lost hubcaps. There are a lot of cars traveling on Highway 99 and some of them lose hubcaps. Nino called to Gus, "Hey Gus, come over here for a minute!"

"What's the matter, Nino?" Gus asked .

"I was polishing a hubcap on this car and it suddenly fell off... and look what was hidden inside!" he answered excitedly.

There on the ground was a little box. It looked like the kind that holds an extra key. Nino reached down and picked it up. Inside was a gold coin.

"Wow! Do you think this belongs to the owner of the car?" Nino asked in a low voice.

"I don't think so," answered Gus. "I remember that the Walrus Falls Museum reported a robbery last month."   [finish the story]

_____

_____

_____

_____

_____

_____

_____

_____
[story title]

All the people in Bovine City had heard about the dognappers. They had heard of missing dogs in Walrus Falls. People in Bovine City reported to the police that their dogs were missing, too. After a few hours, the dog owner would receive a phone call. The voice on the phone always said the same thing. "If you want to see your dog again, leave $500.00 in small bills in locker number 14 at the Bovine City Bus Station." The police investigated, but they could not catch the dognappers.

Ernie Niblit usually left his dog Mylo out in the front yard because he chewed up everything in sight when he was inside the house. Mylo also eats at least three 25-pound bags of dog food every day. When Mylo doesn't get his food, he gets really angry.

Ernie was coming home from work and as he pulled up in front of his house, he couldn't see Mylo. Mylo was missing! [finish the story]

_____

_____

_____

_____

_____

_____

_____

_____

_____

[story title]

Lulu Werble is a member of the Walrus Falls Volunteer Fire Department. She also delivers all the mail, works as a private investigator, and is a former trapeze performer for the Zlinger Brothers Traveling Circus. Lulu was at the fire station inspecting all the fire hoses when a call came to the station. "It's for you, Lulu!" a voice called out. "It's your boss at the Open Eyes Detective Agency. He wants you to come over right away. There is something strange going on at the Lazy B Cattle Ranch. All of the cattle are missing!" [finish the story]

_____
_____
_____
_____
_____
_____
_____
_____
_____
_____
_____
_____
_____
_____

[story title]

Herb Sherbert was going on vacation. He paints the white lines on all the highways for the highway department. He likes to do things on vacation that have nothing to do with painting white lines on highways.

Herb has a dream. He wants to be the first person in the world to row across the Atlantic Ocean. He has been practicing for three years on a lake. Now he is ready for his big trip. As he drove his car toward the coast, he began to think about his dream. "I think I am ready to row across the Atlantic," he said to himself. "I have been practicing for three years. I can't think of anything that could go wrong. I can swim, I have plenty of food and water, and I have a computer that tells me where I am and how far I am from land." **[finish the story]**

_____

_____

_____

_____

_____

_____

_____

_____

_____

_____

_____

_____
[story title]

Nina Spleen was driving home from her job at Nino's Video Store. She was just turning into her driveway when she noticed a huge package sitting on her front steps. It was wrapped in brown paper, and it had a large, red bow on top.

As Nina walked closer to the stairs, she saw that there was a note attached to the top of the package. She tore it off, and began to read.

"You have been selected to receive this free gift from the Loomis Robot Company! That's right...free! Please read the instruction booklet VERY CAREFULLY! Your personal robot is able to do many household tasks that you must do now. Remember to read ALL the instructions before using your robot. [finish the story]

_____
_____
_____
_____
_____
_____
_____
_____
_____
_____
_____

[story title]

Nino Feeney works for the Ajax Pillow and Blanket Company. He has been trying to invent a new pillow for the company. His boss, Harvey Gallop, is always calling him to ask if the new secret Super Pillow is ready. Finally after six months, Nino was ready to show his boss the Super Pillow.

As Mr. Gallop came into Nino's office, Nino was taking the Super Pillow out of a large case. "Here, Mr. Gallop, put the pillow on my desk and sit down. Then put your head down on the pillow and tell me what you think. Mr. Gallop sat down and put his head on the Super Pillow. As Nino searched for some test results, he couldn't wait any longer.

"Well, Mr. Gallop, how do you like it?" he asked hopefully. But there was no answer. There was no answer because Mr. Gallop was fast asleep!

[finish the story]

_____

_____

_____

_____

_____

_____

_____

_____

_____